RAINBOWS OF PROMISE

RAINBOWS OF PROMISE

IVY DUFFY DOHERTY

Review and Herald Publishing Association
Washington, DC 20039-0555
Hagerstown, MD 21740

This book was
Edited by Gerald Wheeler
Designed by Dennis Ferree

R & H Cataloging Service

Doherty, Ivy Duffy, 1922-
Rainbows of promise.

1. Douglass, Frederick, 1817-1895. I. Title.
923.6 [B]

ISBN 0-8280-0213-4

Printed in U.S.A.

RAINBOWS OF PROMISE

Chapter 1

Her hands race like flashes of lightning, 7-year-old Freddie Bailey thought as he watched Grandma Betsy's fingers guide her wooden netting needle in and out, in and out.

"Your fishnet is growing big, Grandma Betsy," he said. "Is it almost finished?"

"Yes," she answered, "it's almost ready for Uncle Turpin to take it with all the other nets I've made since he was here last."

"Where will he sell them?"

"That depends on who ordered them from Old Master," she replied. "I suppose fishermen near where he lives at the Wye River Place will buy them." Then she asked, "Why aren't you in the water cooling off with the other children?" She felt his forehead. "Are you sick? Do you have a fever?"

"I'm all right. I just want to stay here to watch you."

"No harm done if you do," she said, returning to her work.

"Lazy Freddie!" came the shouts from the creek, but the boy made no move to join the other children.

At last he said, "Grandma Betsy?"

"What is it, Freddie? What's on my boy's mind today?"

"I heard Tildy talking about a slave. What's a slave?"

The needle and twine and knobby fingers sped on, and she spoke in that gentle way of hers. "A slave is a worker for Old Master."

"Oh," he said. "Oh."

When his grandmother tucked her needle and twine into the pocket of her calico smock, he helped her roll the net into a neat bundle. The other children came hurrying from the water and scuffled to grab corners of the bundle.

On the trail to the cabin they formed a procession behind the old woman, and while they walked they composed a song. "A net. A net," they sang. "A net for shad. A net for herring. Fishes, come. Fishes, come to the net. Come to the net. Swim to the net, you fishes!"

Grandma Betsy's cabin at the edge of the woods in Tuckahoe, Talbot County, Maryland, had been built long ago of logs. Clay and straw chinked the cracks to keep out the cold. Often she had told her children that it was special, there by itself instead of with all the other cabins at the servants' quarters. She enjoyed its quietness and big open fireplace.

The cabin had no windows, but the glow of the fire gave light on dreary winter days. At night Grandma Betsy lighted a pine torch so she could see to mend clothes or to work on Old Master's nets. She stood the torch in a cracked blue pitcher Freddie had found in the woods. He'd been glad he could give it to her, for it was a way of showing how much he loved her.

Upstairs was the children's sleeping place, the attic floor made into one large bed. Freddie enjoyed climbing the ladder to the sleeping place. "Look, I'm a possum!" he'd sometimes call to Grandma Betsy. Once he fell and hurt himself, but he didn't cry. He wouldn't have the other children laugh at him, and besides, Grandma Betsy said he was too big to cry over what she called "ordinary hurts."

As for the newest fishing net, Grandma Betsy found a place for it with the others outside the cabin door, waiting for Uncle Turpin to come. As soon as Freddie had eaten his lunch—a cold slice of mush left from breakfast—he headed for Mr. Lee's gristmill. No matter how much work the man had to do, he always welcomed Freddie and seemed happy to answer his questions, such as "How does the water turn the big wheel?" or "How can the mill grind the grain?" or "Why does the grain need to be ground?"

Sometimes Grandma Betsy complained that his many questions made her head spin, but they never seemed to bother Mr. Lee. He said asking questions was a good way for a boy to learn, and to learn was very important.

Today Mr. Lee asked, "Would you like to shovel some grain into a sack for me?"

Freddie nodded and smiled. He loved the dusty corn smell, and it made him feel grown up to be helping Mr. Lee.

"When I'm big will you let me work for you?"

"If you were my boy, I'd say Yes, but you're not, and that makes it impossible for me to give you a promise. You're Captain Aaron Anthony's boy."

Dropping his trowel, Freddie stared at his

friend. "I'm Grandma Betsy's boy!" he cried, "and my real mother is Harriet Bailey!"

Mr. Lee went on stacking sacks, but for Freddie the enjoyment of helping had vanished. He wandered outdoors, where he watched the giant mill wheel turn. Sometimes he saw rainbows in the spray that flung away from the wheel into the wind. Grandma Betsy told him the preacher had said rainbows were a wonderful "promise sign," and promise signs were for making people "happy with hoping" and to help them remember that God loves them.

A rainbow flickered in the sunlight. Freddie gazed at it, but it didn't make him feel happy. Who was Captain Anthony? He was sure Grandma Betsy would say Mr. Lee was wrong. "You're *my* boy, Freddie Bailey," she'd say.

As the miller started for home Freddie asked, "Mr. Lee, who is Captain Aaron Anthony?"

"You know that Grandma Betsy and your mother work for someone they call Old Master?" the man replied. "Old Master is the name given Captain Anthony by his workers."

When Freddie had asked Grandma Betsy, "What's a slave?" she had said, "A worker for Old Master." She worked for Old Master. Was *she* a slave? And if he, as Mr. Lee said, belonged to Old Master, was *he* too a slave? And anyway, what did *slave* mean? Grandma Betsy would tell him.

Lying in bed that night, he heard someone calling, "Come quickly, Betsy Bailey. Little Teddy is very sick!"

"I'm ready now, Tildy," the woman answered.

Freddie wished he could be hurrying toward

the quarters through the warm, starry night, his hand clasped in Grandma Betsy's. People said she knew what to do for sicknesses. He had watched her make her own medicines from herbs she'd gathered, and people claimed her poultices and medicines made them well.

Now he remembered the storm of the night before, the jabbing lightning and the fierce thunder that had terrified him. After he'd slid down the ladder, it was magic the way his fear vanished when he saw her calm face. She had put aside the mending of a tow linen shirt to take him on her lap. Snuggling close to her, he thought, my grandma isn't afraid of *anything*, and she won't let anything hurt me.

When Grandma Betsy returned, he joined her on her old gray blanket. "Is Teddy all right?" he asked.

"He's very sick. This time I had to send for Old Master, and he brought the doctor. It took a long time for them to come so far. I hear Mr. Lee's roosters crowing. We must get some sleep. Would you like to stay here with me?"

"Oh, yes," he whispered, slipping his hand in hers.

One morning Freddie sat at the breakfast table staring off into space. "You've been quieter than usual the past few days, Freddie," Grandma Betsy said. "Is something worrying you?"

"Mr. Lee said I belong to Captain Aaron Anthony and that he is Old Master. I don't belong to Captain Anthony, do I? I'm your boy and I'm Harriet's boy, aren't I?"

"Yes, you belong to both of us, but we all belong

to Captain Anthony, even your brother and sisters, and everyone at the quarters, and the children who live in this cabin."

"Will I be a worker for Old Master?" Freddie asked. "Will I have to leave you and live with him?"

"Yes, when you are a little older."

Leave Grandma Betsy! He rebelled at the thought. I won't, he told himself.

Then he went on. "You said a slave is a worker for Old Master. That means we are all slaves?"

"Yes, we're all Old Master's slaves."

"What does *slave* mean?"

"It means you belong to a master and you may do things for yourself only when all that your master wants you to do is done. He tells you what you may eat and wear and where you may go. You don't have a home of your own. Old Master owns all the cabins on this farm."

"But you said our cabin is special," the boy protested.

"Not special in that way, Freddie," she said. "It isn't *my* cabin. Old Master could tell someone else to live in it anytime he wants to."

The boy felt bewildered now. "Was Grandpa Isaac a slave?"

"No, he was a freedman. He didn't belong to anyone. When you're free, you may work and live wherever you choose. Grandpa chose to live here with me."

Grandma Betsy, who *made* slaves?"

"Some people say God did. They tell us He made people with black skins to work for those with white ones."

"Do you think God made black people to be the white people's workers?"

"No, Freddie," she replied, "I don't think the kind God had a hand in such an arrangement. That's only what some people suppose."

Suppose, just suppose, he thought, that God had made black people to be slaves—then how could Grandpa Isaac be black and not a slave? Were there other black people who were not slaves? Would he ever learn all the answers to his questions?

Later that day Uncle Turpin stopped by. "Old Master said for you to get an early start, Betsy Bailey. I wish I could give you a ride on the wagon, but I have Old Master's business to attend to in Hillsboro tomorrow."

Where did Old Master want Grandma Betsy? Fear shot through him. He didn't want her to go anywhere!

In the morning Freddie found her ready to leave for the Wye River Place. The children argued about who would go with her until he announced, "I'm the biggest and the oldest and the strongest. I could walk a hundred miles. *I'm* going with Grandma Betsy!"

"Yes, I'll take Freddie," the old woman said, "seeing he's the oldest. Here's Tildy now, to stay with the rest of you for the day."

The boy had never known such happiness, for Grandma Betsy would be his for a whole day. He need not share her with the other children or with her work. Never had he felt so close to her. As she walked, she seemed to drag him along. "It's a long way. How much farther do we have to go?" he complained at last. "I'm thirsty and hungry and hot and tired!"

But there, finally, was the Wye River Place.

Hounds barked and children rushed about, shouting and squealing. "I didn't know there could be so many children!" the boy whispered. And the houses were so big, especially compared with the little cabin at Tuckahoe.

Men and women worked in the fields with shovels, rakes, hoes and wheelbarrows, tending patches of melons. Shrill laughter, shouting, singing and hurrying all mingled together. The bigness and movement and noise suddenly made him wish he hadn't wanted to come to the Wye River Place.

Chapter 2

A mob of children swarmed around him. "Little baby, want to fight with me?" a tall boy demanded.

And a girl tugged his hair. "Baby curls!" she teased. "Does your grandma put curling rags in your hair to make it so pretty?"

"Come, now! That's no way to treat Freddie!" Grandma Betsy interrupted. "Look, Freddie, here is your brother, Perry, and your sisters Eliza and Sarah. Play with them while I go to talk to Aunt Katy and Old Master."

"Come, play," Perry invited. "I won't let anyone tease you." But Freddie was too shy to join them. He watched the others for what seemed a long time. After a while he began to wonder what was keeping Grandma Betsy.

Suddenly a girl came running. "Your grandma's gone!" she cried. "She's gone without you. You're to stay here with us now!"

"Grandma Betsy wouldn't go home without me!"

"Ask Aunt Katy," the girl said. "She's in the kitchen."

A deep, hurting pain from not knowing what was taking place flooded him. He ran into the kitchen. "What do you think you're doing, breaking into my kitchen like a whirlwind?" stormed someone who no doubt was Aunt Katy, her face clouded with anger.

"I want Grandma Betsy!" he wailed. "I want to go home with her!"

"This is your home now!" the woman shouted. "You'll be staying right here! You'll mind what Aunt Katy tells you, and you won't fret for your grandma. Old Master says you're to live here, and here you stay."

"I want Grandma Betsy!" Freddie pleaded. Dashing outdoors, he raced blindly across the yard. Which way had they come? Everywhere he turned he saw buildings and trails and fences and flowers and trees, and he could not tell from which direction they had traveled.

"Don't cry, little Freddie," Sarah said. "We'll look after you."

"Grandma Betsy brought us here, too," Perry added, "and it's sad for her to leave her children."

"She'll come back for me!" Freddie cried.

"I don't believe she will," Perry replied. "Old Master told her to bring you, and she must do as he says."

The slave boy stopped his weeping. "I'll find my way back home!"

That night at suppertime Freddie was too lonely to take a single bite of his corn bread. "All right, young man," snapped Aunt Katy. "If that's the way you want it, that's the way it will be. You can just go to bed hungry."

His sleeping place was a big closet. Aunt Katy handed him a ragged blanket and said, "Now, not another squeak out of you."

In his sorrow a glimmer of understanding of what Grandma Betsy had meant by not crying over ordinary hurts came to him. Falling from a ladder was nothing compared with the agony of separation from her. And he remembered now his thought that she would not let anything hurt him. He began to see that Grandma Betsy would have no choice in what happened to him. No, she must do, instead, what Old Master told her. Was that also what being a slave meant?

"Now," Aunt Katy announced in the morning, "I am in charge in Old Master's kitchen. You do as I tell you, and you must mind your manners, Frederick Augustus Washington Bailey. Call Old Master's children Master and Miss, and you'll do anything his daughter, Miss Lucretia, orders. Understand? Never go to the Great House. I'll take the skin off you if I hear of such a thing. You'll keep the yard beyond the kitchen clean and make sure the chickens stay out of my garden. At milking time you'll drive the cows from pasture and then back again, and you'll do anything else I have a mind to tell you. That clear?"

"Yes, Aunt Katy." But could he remember all that she had ordered?

"Now," she said, giving him a shove, "find where everyone and everything is so you won't get lost when you're sent on errands."

Freddie spotted his sister Sarah weeding a flower bed. "Our mother will visit us sometime," she said. "She comes on her rest days or when she can get a ride. It's a long way for her when she has to walk."

"You, Sarah Bailey, get to work!" Aunt Katy yelled. "Freddie Bailey, move on!"

He wandered toward the pasture, all the while watching for a chance to slip away to Grandma Betsy. Suddenly three boys dashed toward him and grabbed the front of his shirt.

"Hello, baby!" one of them hissed. "We came to teach you how to grow up fast!"

"See how we'll teach you?" a second boy said, slapping his face.

Freddie cried out in pain. I'll tell Grandma Betsy, he thought. She'll punish them.

"And this is another way we'll teach you," the third boy added, delivering a sharp kick to each of Freddie's shins. Through stinging tears Freddie saw another figure running toward them, and he stared in fascination. It was the first time he had ever seen a white child.

"You ruffians!" the newcomer exclaimed. "Leave that little fellow alone! I've a good mind to tell Captain Anthony to whip you."

The three slave children slunk away, and the boy said, "You're Freddie Bailey, from Tuckahoe, aren't you?"

Shy and not knowing how to address a white child, Freddie remained silent.

"Are you all right?" the boy asked. Freddie nodded. "Good. You tell me if they are mean to you again. I'm Daniel Lloyd, from the Great House," he went on. "I'll show you around the place so you'll know where everything is."

As they walked, Freddie had his first sight of the Great House, which stood in a beautiful setting of lawns, hedges, trees, and bright flowers. Suddenly he remembered that Aunt Katy had told him not to go near it. But I don't care about Aunt Katy, he told himself. I want to see everything and learn everything!

As Daniel, guiding him, explained about the uses of the many buildings, Freddie wondered how he would keep everything straight in his mind. Now perhaps he understood how he made Grandma Betsy's head spin with his many questions.

"My father has several big farms, and he has men to oversee them," the white lad said. "Captain Anthony is the manager of the overseers, and my father, Colonel Lloyd, is Captain Anthony's master."

"Then Captain Anthony's his slave?"

"No, the captain isn't a slave."

"Well," Freddie said, puzzled, "he works for your father, and workers are slaves."

"Not all workers are slaves," Daniel tried to explain. "Captain Anthony is free. He chooses to work for my father and may leave any time he wishes. A slave can't do that."

Grandpa Isaac was black, yet he was a freedman. Captain Anthony was white, and he worked for Colonel Lloyd, but he was not a slave. Freddie shook his head. Would he ever understand about workers and slaves?

Freddie noticed a darkly woodod place that looked familiar. Was that the way he and Grandma Betsy had come? He'd try to find the way from Aunt Katy's kitchen to those woods, and then he'd be on the trail to Tuckahoe.

When the new morning arrived, Freddie woke

up too late to search for the trail. Aunt Katy's temper matched the heat of the September day. "Get down to the Long Green to swim, and let me be!" she shrieked.

There Freddie saw a big boat lying at anchor, a smaller craft tied to its stern. Men were working aboard it, and swimming to shore was Daniel.

"Why aren't you in the water, Freddie?" the boy greeted him as he scrambled ashore.

"I want to look at the boat," Freddie answered, his eagerness overcoming his shyness.

"That's the *Sally Lloyd*. See, the name is printed across the stern."

A throb of envy shot through the slave boy. Would he ever be able, like Daniel, to look at such printing and tell what it meant?

"Tomorrow Captain Auld will take peaches and melons to Baltimore on the *Sally Lloyd*," Daniel said. "He takes all kinds of things we grow here when they are ready." Then he told how his father and other farmers sent grain to Baltimore to load aboard ships bound for the West Indies.

Freddie wished he could see those great ships. Was wishing a kind of rainbow thing like the preacher had told Grandma Betsy? Hoping?

"What is *hoping?*" he asked.

Daniel laughed. "There hasn't ever been another boy at Aunt Katy's kitchen who has been so full of questions as you, Freddie. Hoping is kind of having deep wishes and believing they can come true."

On the way back to Aunt Katy's kitchen, Daniel told about the Chesapeake Bay, across which the *Sally Lloyd* sailed to Baltimore, and about the brown-skined people, Indians, who had lived around the bay and traveled on its waters before white people had come to live in Maryland. The Indians, he said, had shown the white people how to get food from the bay.

"How do you know so much?" Freddie asked.

"Mr. Page teaches school at the Great House, and I read and keep my ears and eyes open. The map I'll bring will show you Maryland and the Chesapeake Bay." He went on to tell of Captain John Smith, who'd traveled the bay before the first Grandfather Lloyd had come from Wales to make a new home on the Wye River. Captain Smith had made maps, Daniel said, and he and the Indians had been friends.

"I wish Mr. Page would teach me," Freddie stated. "Could you teach me to read?"

"My father wouldn't be pleased if I did."

Why, Freddie wondered, should it be all right for him to learn to read, but not for *me*? "Do you think if someone tried to teach me, I could learn?"

"Of course you could. Any boy whose mind is so full of questions is sure to be able to learn quickly."

At the garden gate a tall slave boy stopped them. "You're little Freddie from Tuckahoe, aren't you? I'm your cousin, Tom. I lived with Grandma Betsy, and now Old Master sends me on the *Sally Lloyd* as Captain Auld's cabin boy. Now I don't have to stay with Aunt Katy anymore. I go to Baltimore."

The children swarmed around Tom, who, drawing a trumpet from behind him, blew a shocking blast of noise. The children laughed and squealed, and Aunt Katy yelled out to them, "You get that wicked thing out of here!"

Big Tom then told of what he'd seen in Baltimore: sailing ships, steamboats, frigates, barges, a stagecoach, marching soldiers, big houses, fireworks. He had heard church bells ringing, and there were thousands of people everywhere.

I'll ask Captain Auld to take me to Baltimore, Freddie said to himself.

Chapter 3

One day Daniel took Freddie to Uncle Abel's shoe shop, which made the slaves' footwear, then to the carpenter's shop, the stables, the storehouses, and the tobacco sheds. But most intriguing to Freddie was the blacksmith's shop, with its glowing forge, the clang of the hammer on the anvil, and the sizzling of hot metal plunged into cold water. The blacksmith produced pots and pans, bolts and wheel rims, and dozens of horseshoes. When Daniel told Freddie that Uncle Tony pulled the aching teeth of slaves with some of his blacksmith tools, the slave boy said, "I think we'd better go now, Daniel!"

On the way back to the kitchen they met Captain Anthony. "So you're Freddie Bailey, my boy from Tuckahoe! And I must say you're a very handsome young man," he added. "Do you think you'll remember where everything is, seeing Master Daniel has been so kind as to guide you around the plantation?"

"I don't know," Freddie replied shyly. "There are so many places to remember."

"You'll do fine. I can tell you're a smart boy. But you must obey Aunt Katy," he added. "Remember that, and you'll stay out of trouble."

When Freddie returned to Aunt Katy's kitchen, she was waiting to pounce on him. "Aunt Katy's not blind!" she scolded. "No supper for disobedient boys!"

That evening she cut thick slices of corn bread for all the children except him. "None for you," she said, tight-lipped. "Boys who go to the Great House don't get supper. If you keep going there, one time you'll stay so long you'll have to come home in the dark. A ghost from the burying ground will come out moaning and grab you."

"Master Daniel said there's no such thing as a ghost," he said, surprised at himself for talking back to Aunt Katy.

"He wasn't giving you the truth," Aunt Katy argued. "There are many at the quarters who've seen them. All dressed in long white robes, they were, and some on huge black horses. Some at the quarters have seen balls of fire fall in that burying ground. And they've heard the most chilling sounds!"

She shook her big fist. "You get out of my kitchen and not a whimper from you about no food."

Outdoors, Freddie heard singing coming from the quarters, and mingled with it he heard shouting, but it didn't take his mind from Aunt Katy. Tears of anger, mixed with those of loneliness for his beloved Grandma Betsy, stung his cheeks. And he felt extremely hungry.

The evening chill forced him back indoors. Sitting on a bench in the chimney corner, he stared into the fire. Suddenly the kitchen door opened, and in walked a tall, beautiful black woman. Someone from the quarters to see Aunt Katy, he supposed.

Aunt Katy's hands went to her hips, and her eyes glittered. "So it's you, Harriet Bailey," she snarled. "Come to see your boy, and he's his mother's boy, I declare. Too good for kitchen and field hands. Just good enough for the company of the young master. Don't you see him there?" She flounced angrily out of the kitchen.

Harriet Bailey sat down beside him. Her arms went around him, and she buried her face in his tangled hair. "My Freddie!" she said. "My boy!" Then she held him away, searching his face. "Freddie, why are you alone when the other children are already in bed?"

Briefly he told of his punishment. "Never you mind about Katy," she said. "I have something special for my hungry boy."

With a smile she drew from her smock pocket a heart-shaped ginger cake. His mouth watered at the first smell of it. "Mrs. Stewart, the overseer's wife, made cakes for me to bring to each of my children," his mother explained.

Freddie gazed deeply into her eyes as he ate, and he thought her the most beautiful mother a boy could ever have. He felt warm with love toward her. *His* mother!

The two glanced up as Aunt Katy stalked into the kitchen, her big ring of keys jingling in her apron pocket.

"Katy, what is the meaning of this? No supper! I'm sure the child doesn't get enough to cure his hunger as it is. I'll tell Old Master what you have done to him!"

"Not even being a common field hand could change you, Princess Harriet," the woman sneered. "Always Old Master's favored one. The one someone secretly taught to read. Your boy disobeyed. After all, he *is* a *slave!*"

"Punish him if he's disobedient," Harriet returned, "but not with the cruelty of hunger." She rocked him gently on her lap and sang about ships on the bay with their sails rosy in the sunset wind.

When morning came, Freddie couldn't remember having seen his mother leave. Had her coming been a marvelous dream? No, for there beside his sleeping place rested a piece of the precious ginger cake that he had saved for today.

Then he remembered something. Aunt Katy had said his mother had been taught to read. Old Master? Or his wife, maybe? Had his mother once worked in Captain Anthony's home? Then another thought took shape. Was Aunt Katy mean to him because she disliked his mother?

That afternoon the boy took Miss Lucretia a message from Aunt Katy. "So you're Freddie," she said with a gentle smile. "My father was right. You are a handsome boy."

Freddie stared at the carpet, and his bashfulness would not let him look at her. "Don't be afraid," she said. "I like little boys."

His next errand took him to Uncle Abel's shop to deliver a package from Captain Anthony, and in his usual way of wanting to know everything, he loitered to find out about making shoes.

"You get on back to Aunt Katy's kitchen, you young nuisance!" Ike, Uncle Abel's shop boy, shouted at him.

"I want to learn about shoes."

"Get!" Ike bellowed. "None of that back talk here!"

When Freddie didn't move, Ike threatened, "I'll teach you to listen!" Picking up an iron rod, he hit Freddie across the forehead. "There! Now you'll know when you're not wanted!"

Terrified, with blood oozing from the wound, Freddie raced to the kitchen. Aunt Katy had no sympathy. "No doubt you got what you deserved. Don't come running to me!"

A maid appeared and led Freddie to Miss Lucretia. "I heard your crying," the maid told him, "and I saw you hurrying to the kitchen."

Lucretia Auld washed away the blood stains and cleaned the wound. Then she dipped a soft cloth in balsam and wound it about his head. Her kindness and the perfume that floated from her rustling dress comforted him.

"I heard you singing when you drove the cows to be milked yesterday," she commented as she bandaged him. "I liked your song about shad and herring. Could you sing it for me?"

Could he sing without choking on the words? But she'd been kind and he'd try to please her. "A net. A net . . . "

"That was delightful," she said when he finished. "It deserves a buttery biscuit!"

After that, when Freddie felt extra hungry, he'd sing under the parlor window. Miss Lucretia would look out with a pleased smile and say, "I think you deserve a piece of bread and butter."

The more Daniel told Freddie of the things Mr.

Page taught him, the more the boy yearned to go to school. When he noticed that the overseers' children also left the plantation to attend school, he couldn't stand it any longer.

His words came tumbling out one morning. "Aunt Katy, I want to go to school!"

The woman rocked with mirthless laughter. "Silly boy! Don't you know you'll never be allowed to go to Mr. Page or attend school with the overseers' children? All you'll ever be taught is work!"

"Master Daniel said he was sure I could learn to read."

"You stupid boy! Master Daniel didn't mean a word of what he said. You should be thinking of what it will be like weeding and hoeing and straining your back. Now, no more school talk!"

Somehow I'll find out how to read! he vowed to himself. I'll learn to read *Sally Lloyd* on a boat. I promise!

Promise? That was a rainbow word. A *hoping* word. Grandma Betsy had always gathered her children together and prayed, "Help my children to be good and kind today, to love one another." I can make prayers like those the preacher taught Grandma Betsy to say, he thought. And he prayed, "Help me to learn to read." There, now, Aunt Katy was wrong! Wait and see.

When he had finished his breakfast, Aunt Katy ordered, "Get your chores done in a hurry and off you go—all of you—to Uncle Copper."

"Uncle Copper teaches us things he's learned from the preacher," Sarah explained to him.

The children were scrubbed and in clean

clothes when Aunt Katy shook her finger at them. "Now mind your manners," she said. "Uncle Copper is particular."

Uncle Copper sat at his cabin door, his crutches beside him, and beside them three hickory sticks. Seeing them, Freddie remembered Aunt Katy's words "Uncle Copper is particular."

The children gathered around the brown, wrinkled man. Eyeing the hickory sticks, Freddie crept to safety behind Perry.

"We'll work again on the Lord's Prayer," Uncle Copper announced. "Kneel down, close your eyes, and not one twitter out of anyone. Say everything after me: 'Our Father which art—' There, you!" He poked a child with a skinny finger. "Shut both those wandering eyes! '. . . which art in heaven, hallowed be thy—' *Now there,* you new one. It's Freddie, isn't it? The boy from Tuckahoe. You talk up, and don't hide. 'Thy kingdom come—' You, there! Don't yawn while we're praying." He switched the boy lightly with one of the hickory sticks.

Freddie became utterly confused about which words he should repeat after Uncle Copper and which he should ignore. How did all the others know what they should be saying?

"Now we must begin all over again," Uncle Copper said. "None of you paid enough attention. And *you,* stop your pushing!"

The lesson ended, and Freddie left puzzled.

As the weeks went by, he was almost always hungry, even reduced to wrestling with the dog for scraps of food from Captain Anthony's table. At the slave quarters, the older ones gave him some of their food. "Little ones need more to eat than we do," they told him.

One day he asked Daniel why it was difficult for him to understand the language some of the people in the slave quarters spoke.

"Slaves came originally from Africa," the white boy explained. "Their parents or their grandparents spoke different languages. Gradually they have mixed them until they have invented a language of their own."

"You said *Africa?*" Freddie asked.

"Yes, it's another land far across the ocean. You know Grandma Arlie at the quarters? She came from Africa. Father says no one knows her age, but he is sure she is very old. She's been with the Lloyd families for many years. My father told her she could live in our house with the other servants or she could have a cabin of her own now that she is too old to work, but no, she wishes to be with her friends and family at the quarters."

Chapter 4

"One night," Daniel recounted, "when the people in Grandma Arlie's African village were making music and dancing, strange men pounced upon the young people. They chained them all together and marched them to the ocean, where they sold them to a ship captain, who loaded them aboard. Some of the slaves grew ill and died on the way, and when the rest of them finally reached our country, plantation owners bought them to work on the farms and in the houses. That is how one of my grandfathers obtained Grandma Arlie."

The story made the slave boy feel sad.

"Mr. Page said there have always been slaves," Daniel continued, "almost as long as people have lived in the world. Some people have been masters and have bought their slaves to do their work, or they have stolen them."

"Did Grandma Arlie say she was lonely and unhappy to be stolen away from her mother and father?" Freddie asked.

"No, but I know how I'd feel if someone took me away from my home."

"I miss Grandma Betsy, so *I* know how she felt," Freddie sighed.

One day he asked Grandma Arlie, "Why do some of Colonel Lloyd's or Captain Anthony's families come to the meetings when the preacher talks to the slaves?"

"I suppose they fear that when we get together we'll make plans to run away," she said. "But here's one who couldn't go, and wouldn't if she could. This Wye River Place has been my home for long years, and the people of the Great House have been most kind to me. And besides, where would I go?"

At the quarters Freddie heard conversations about God. People said that God is love, that He is good. That being so, he thought, Grandma Betsy must have been correct when she had said the kind God would not have made anyone to be a slave.

Often, early in the morning, he heard the blast of the overseer's horn calling the workers to the fields, and he'd seen the stern-faced overseer, whip in hand, riding among them.

He knew well the sounds of the return of the slaves to their quarters at nightfall: the sad singing, tired talk and laughter, the braying of mules, the jingle of harness. Sometimes he managed to steal away from Aunt Katy to sit with his friends there, to enjoy the cheery evening fires and to listen to their talk and singing.

One morning sobbing in the kitchen awakened him. Then he heard a man's voice. "That will teach you to disobey me, Esther Bailey! How many times have I told you not to go with Ned? He belongs to Colonel Lloyd, and you belong here. You understand?"

"I'll promise not to see Ned again, Old Master,"

the boy's aunt Esther, still weeping, replied. Freddie heard Captain Anthony leave, and then Aunt Katy burst into the kitchen. "Serves you right for Old Master to whip you good and hard," the woman sneered. "You disobey, what do you expect he'll do? He can't have disobedience, can he?"

Freddie drew his ancient blanket about his shoulders. Did Aunt Esther deserve the whipping? Was Aunt Katy right?

The children were eating their morning mush when Big Tom rushed into the kitchen. "Did you hear, Aunt Katy? Aunt Jenny and Uncle Noah have gone!"

"Gone?" Katy asked, staring. "What do you mean, 'gone,' Big Tom?"

"No one can find them," he said, still puffing. "It seems they crept away in the night. Disappeared. Vanished. No one knows where they are."

Aunt Katy sat heavily on the bench in the chimney corner. She stared at Big Tom a moment, then smiled. "They'll be back," she declared. "I can promise you that. Old Master will get the patrollers to search for them. You see if he doesn't! And there are the hounds . . ."

"They might be a long way by now, Aunt Katy," Big Tom argued. "The forests and hills and swamps and even the bay will help hide them. If they move carefully during the night and hide in the daylight, maybe they'll be fortunate and get away to the North. Maybe to safe Canada."

Aunt Katy sprang from the bench, grasping his shoulders with her large hands. "How do you know about the North, Big Tom?" she demanded. "How do you know about Canada?"

"Calm down, Aunt Katy," he said, drawing away from her. He laughed then. "How do I know about the North and Canada? Don't be silly, Aunt Katy. Don't I go to Baltimore, where I can see and hear things?"

Freddie, taking the cows to pasture that frosty autumn morning, forgot briefly his cracked and bleeding feet that had suffered from the recent cold days. His thoughts continued to haunt him—thoughts of all that he had just heard in the kitchen.

Why did Aunt Esther allow Old Master to beat her? Was there nothing she, a grown woman, could do? Couldn't she snatch the whip away from him? Run from him? Or was it true that she really deserved the punishment? Why had Aunt Jenny and Uncle Noah disappeared? Where were they now? Who were the patrollers? And what was that about the hounds? Daniel had faced north once, he recalled, but how does one start north and keep going in that direction when there are trees and hills and water in the way?

Then he smiled. "When I'm big, if anyone whips me I'll run away!" he told himself.

Before suppertime he found Big Tom. "Tell me about the North and Canada," he begged.

"You're too young to understand."

"Please, Big Tom."

"If you give me the corn bread you get for your supper, I'll tell you."

Already his stomach growled from emptiness, and the thought of corn bread made his mouth water, but he wanted to know about the North and Canada more than he wanted food.

"All right," he said, "I'll promise to give you my

piece of corn bread."

Big Tom laughed and patted the boy's shoulder. "If a slave can run away and get to New York or Massachusetts or Canada, that's the North." He pointed in the same direction as Daniel had indicated as being north. "Then if he's careful he doesn't have to be a slave anymore. He's *free*, and he can do what he wants.

"But remember," he continued, "he has to be careful, because the masters who own slaves have notices printed in newspapers and placed on buildings. They describe whom the runaways belong to, what they look like, whether they have any scars on them, how old they are, and where the master thinks they might be trying to go. And the masters usually promise to give the finder a reward—that's money—if he can bring their slaves back to them or tell them where they are.

"And even if you aren't a runaway, but really a freedman in the North, someone might grab you and sell you if he finds you're not carrying papers that show you are free. And I've heard talk in Baltimore," Tom added, "that masters try to get the freed slaves to go back to Africa so they won't be working to get all the other slaves to run away."

"How do you know what's on signs and in newspapers when you can't read?"

"I hear people talking," Tom said. "I listen and I learn, and I have friends who can read things to me. I know about slave-auction signs and notices, too. They tell about slaves that are to be sold—how many, at what place and what time, how old they are, and what jobs they can——"

Aunt Katy's yelling for the children to eat

supper interrupted him. He cupped the boy's chin in his hand, tilted his face, and looked into his eyes. "I don't want your corn bread, little Freddie," he said. "I get enough to eat, and I know Aunt Katy is kind of mean to you. You have the corn bread. And don't talk about what I told you. Not to anyone, understand?"

"I promise," Freddy said, then added, "I like you, Big Tom!"

Two weeks passed, and the runaways had still not returned.

"Why are so many carts coming from everywhere today?" he asked Daniel.

The master's son explained that during the last two days of each month men arrived from the outlying farms to get food supplies for all the workers. "Do you remember that Uncle Turpin brought food to your Grandma Betsy?" Daniel reminded him.

Grandma Betsy? He wondered what she was doing. Did she miss him as much as he did her?

Freddie enjoyed lingering about the stables to watch the "hands" groom the horses. Sometimes they allowed him to help clean the troughs and fill them with fresh water.

He couldn't understand why Old Barney, the slave in charge of the stables, could never fully please the people from the Great House. It always seemed that one or another of the Lloyd family would complain that he'd done poor work. Why, the boy wondered, didn't Barney tell them that he'd tried to do his very best work? Did he never defend himself because he belonged to Colonel Lloyd? Was that also a part of being a slave?

One afternoon he saw Colonel Lloyd whip the old slave. Would anyone whip me, Freddie thought, even when I did my very best?

The weather had turned fiercely cold, making him long for the comforts of the Tuckahoe cabin and Grandma Betsy. In the cold season Grandma Betsy had not insisted that her children go outdoors. The boy had no choice now.

Every once in a while Freddie wondered why he hadn't put more effort into returning to Tuckahoe. Was it because there was so much happening at the Wye River Place all the time? Was it that there were new things occurring for him to learn about every day? Or was it a fear that if he started out he'd become lost along the way? A fear of patrollers and bloodhounds? Perry had told him bloodhounds were mighty clever about picking up the scent of a person. Did Miss Lucretia with her kindness keep him there? Or Daniel, always answering his questions?

Freddie watched visitors by the dozen arrive in carriages and on horseback at the Great House. "They'll be hunting foxes," Big Tom told him. On that day of chilling wind and leaden sky the hunting party scattered across the fields.

Freddie heard the squall of a hunted fox, and with fists clenched and heart thumping against his ribs he remembered all too clearly Aunt Katy's talk about the hounds' ability to scent Aunt Jenny and Uncle Noah. She'd sometimes even threatened to have *him* chased by bloodhounds.

That night he listened, hoping to hear the call of the fox still in freedom, but all that came to him was the sigh of the wind.

Snow flew. The people at the Great House began the flutter of Christmas preparations: marvelous-smelling foods, bright lights, the yule log carried in, company arriving, dancing and music. And Aunt Katy did her share of preparing wonderful food for Captain Anthony's family. In turn the master sent cheese and candies to his kitchen children.

Chapter 5

"I don't know what Christmas means," Freddie confided to Daniel one day.

"You know who God is?"

"Yes," the slave boy replied. "He is love and He is good."

Surprise filled Daniel's voice. "You're the only child of your kind Aunt Katy has ever had at her kitchen!"

"And she's sorry she has me," Freddie commented.

"I think you're right about that, but that isn't important. God sent His Son to this world. His name was Jesus, and He came as a little baby to live with Joseph and Mary. We have Christmas as a happy time to remember Jesus' birthday. He came to this earth to show people how to live, how to love and be kind to one another, and not to hate or be unkind. Every Christmas we remember His birthday by giving presents to others."

Freddie wondered how Jesus taught people to be kind. Did He eat good-smelling food while others went hungry? Did he have warm clothing while others shivered? Or did He share what He had?

RAINBOWS OF PROMISE

One spring day Aunt Katy said, "Old Master sent for you to come to his house, Freddie Bailey. What mischief have you been into now?

As he scurried to the brick house by the river his heart beat fearfully, What, indeed, had he done?

There smiling, gentle Lucretia Auld put her arm about his shoulders. "I have a wonderful surprise for you, Freddie. Captain Anthony is going to let you sail to Baltimore with my husband, Captain Auld, on the *Sally Lloyd*, and you'll live with my husband's brother, Hugh Auld."

Freddie was wild with excitement until Miss Lucretia decided that he must be scrubbed clean. Would she rub his skin away? But to his joy he received his first pair of linsey-woolsey trousers.

In the pearl light of dawn the *Sally Lloyd* moved with the current into the broad waters of Chesapeake Bay. Ropes groaned and sails flapped. Gulls soared overhead, and Freddie felt a bursting excitement after the first gloom of leaving his friends and brother and sisters.

Watching the spray as the sloop nosed its way through the vast waters, he recalled Mr. Lee's mill. Then the gold of the sunrise burst across the flung waters to create a magnificent rainbow. Freddie reminded himself that he'd wished for something as important as going to Baltimore, and now it was really happening! Was that what Grandma Betsy's preacher meant by being "happy with hoping"?

And on top of his happiness, he realized that Aunt Katy was not around to yell at him not to fall off the *Sally Lloyd*.

The door to Hugh Auld's house opened to the knock of Rich, the sloop hand. There stood Hugh,

Sophia, and their little son, Tommy. "I want you to be kind to Tommy," Miss Sophia said, "and take good care of him."

For the first time in his life Freddie would live in a real home. A little kitchen loft would be his very own room, with a bed and a covering on the floor. But above all else, the Auld house had books and newspapers.

That night, lying on his straw-filled mattress, Freddie felt rich, and he wondered why, of all Aunt Katy's children, the master had chosen him to come to Baltimore.

In the morning he gazed through the windows at the tall masts and spars in the distance at the waterfront. After getting up he put on one of the new suits of clothes Miss Sophia had made him.

When Hugh had left for his shipyard and Sophia finished morning chores, she sat with Tommy and Freddie to teach them the shepherd's psalm. Freddie listened, entranced, while she explained the meaning of the words. And then she went on to tell the story of the Good Shepherd, who searched until He found His little lost lamb.

Every day Miss Sophia allowed Freddie to make short trips to the waterfront and to town. That way he could learn where things were when she and her husband sent him on errands. After each adventure he returned to tell shyly of all he had seen and heard. He enjoyed watching the comings and goings of the ships on the bay and hearing the swivel gun firing its loud signal for the departure of the steamboats. And at night he drank in every word as Hugh talked about his shipyard, which was small but would grow.

Freddie heard Sophia tell Hugh, "There never was a child like him, husband. Such a mind for learning, and such a hunger for it."

Since his arrival in Baltimore he had longed to handle a book—to open its covers and see the printing. His opportunity came when Miss Sophia went to a ladies' meeting at her church, leaving Tommy in his care. Opening a book, the slave boy leafed through it and sighed. If only he could learn what all those marks and lines and squiggles meant.

Later one night Freddie awoke to the sound of angry voices. "You're too nice to the child, Sophia," he heard Hugh say. "You don't know how to treat a slave!"

"That is correct, husband," his wife answered. "For one thing, he's such a beautiful child, and for another, I am positive his mind is capable of great things. When I look at him, I remember how I felt to be a working girl, a weaver, a *nothing*. All I wanted was to be treated with kindness and respect, and I've decided I'll do for this child what I wish someone had done for me."

His voice grew harsher. "You don't know what you're saying, woman!"

"Don't worry," his wife replied. "I know he's a slave, but I have no notions about my being a slaveholder."

Trembling, Freddie pulled his quilt over his head so he wouldn't hear their quarrel.

The next morning Tommy practiced the alphabet. "*A* is for *anchor*," Sophia said, and Tommy repeated, "*A* is for *anchor*."

"What else?" his mother asked.

"*Apple,* and *ant,* and *anchor,*" Tommy recited, then added, "I saw a big anchor down at the wharf yesterday. Freddie did too, didn't you, Freddie?"

The slave boy pressed close to Mrs. Auld. "Yes," he said, his smile still shy, "and I heard some of the men talking about a ship that arrived from the West Indies and brought sugar to Baltimore. Master Daniel told me about the big ships that come to Chesapeake Bay from the Indies."

"You're clever, remembering that," the woman said with a delighted smile.

"Miss Sophia," he ventured, "could you teach me *A, B, C?*"

"Of course I could teach you! Time for our Bible lesson now, and we'll learn the Lord's Prayer. You say after me, 'Our Father which art in heaven——' "

" 'Hallowed be thy name. Thy kingdom come,' " Freddie added.

"Freddie, where did you hear that?" she exclaimed.

"Uncle Copper taught us lots of things, but I always stood behind Perry when we went to Uncle Copper for lessons, so he couldn't reach me to switch me with a hickory stick."

One day Hugh came home to find the lessons in progress. "Hugh, dear, I have a wonderful surprise for you," Sophia announced. "Listen. Tell Master Hugh what K stands for, Freddie."

The boy immediately caught the glint of anger in Hugh Auld's eyes. He knew that expression, for he'd seen such displeasure in the eyes of Colonel Lloyd when he had whipped Old Barney and when Old Master had been angry with him when he'd neglected chores or had been in some mischief.

"K is for *kite* and *kitten* and *kitchen*——"

Hugh grabbed Freddie from beside his wife and, shoving him across the room, demanded, "Sophia, won't you *ever* understand your place or the boy's?"

"What harm can I do?" she returned. "Soon I'll have him reading the Bible, and surely he can only be a better person for that."

His laughter was hard and cold. "What harm? I'll tell you what harm: He'll read about Moses and his leading the Israelites out of slavery. And he'll read the teachings of Jesus. They are more dangerous for a slave to learn than any Declaration of Independence, or if he knew everything the newspapers have in them about freedom. And besides, if he learns to read he'll be able to write his own passes. Then he'd be gone in a flash."

"But he's such a *knowing* little boy, Hugh, and full of promise!" his wife protested.

"That's what I'm trying to tell you! Anyone can see he's full of promise. That's why I forbid you to give him another lesson."

"But Hugh——"

"No more!" he yelled.

Freddie crept outdoors, feeling that his heart had cracked wide open from disappointment. He could still hear angry voices.

"It's unlawful for you to teach a slave to read," Hugh Auld continued.

"Not in Maryland!" Sophia countered.

"There'd be no holding him if these lessons were to continue," her husband went one. "He'd be dissatisified, unhappy. What you should be doing is training him to be a hardworking, money-earning slave. You give a slave reading and writing and you've given him his freedom!"

For Freddie a marvelous door had closed in one flash of angry exhange. And although Tommy begged for his company at lesson time, Sophia remained firm. "We must obey your papa," she said. In the future the slave boy must go get bread from the bakery during Tommy's lessons.

At the shipyard the carpenters marked their timbers for the ship they were building: *L* for larboard, *S* for starboard. And he copied other letters on waste timber with pieces of charcoal. When he met a friendly child on the street, he'd show his wooden "slate" and say, pointing, "That's *S* and that's *LA* and that's *LF*."

Then the child would boast, "I know others that you don't have there. See, this is *B*, and *D*, and *Z*."

He practiced his writing on fences and walls and pavement. And when Sophia wasn't present, he'd copy from *Webster's Spelling Book* until soon he could write all the letters of the alphabet without looking at the book.

Flashes of conversation kept coming back to him, such as "You give a slave reading and writing, and you've given him his freedom." He didn't understand the exact meaning of those words, but he sensed that they had some special importance in his life.

All of Sophia's snatching away of reading material and all her uneasy watchfulness only stirred Freddie's desire for learning. He'd discover his own ways to educate himself.

Much of the happiness seemed to have vanished from the Auld home now. Miss Sophia's once-pretty face grew strained, Freddie thought, as though something had closed inside her and she'd never be able to open it again. Desperately he tried to please her, to put her at ease about her denial of his most cherished wish, but he failed.

Soon he made friends with two white boys, William and Henry, who lived on Philpot Street. After he had finished his errands and chores he'd take his copy of the spelling book and ask them, "What is this word?" At home he'd go over what they'd taught him until he had fixed it in his mind.

He thought much about Sophia. She was another person who could not do what she wished. Master Hugh had seen to that. Was she his slave? Did Hugh Auld own her, as Captain Anthony did him?

When Sophia took Tommy to his first day at school, Freddie felt an indescribable ache deep inside him. Why? Why? He could almost burst from wanting to know why Tommy could go to school while he could not.

One day Rich, the sloop hand from the *Sally Lloyd*, came to tell the Aulds that Captain Anthony had died and that Freddie must return for the settlement of the master's estate. The court would divide it between Miss Lucretia and Master Andrew, the only relatives.

"You mean Freddie is to be *sold!*" Sophia gasped.

"Not if Miss Lucretia can help it," Rich said. "She's always favored him."

Fear gripped the boy, for he'd heard, especially on the waterfront, frightening stories about the sale of slaves.

"Please, let me not be sold!" he prayed often.

The settlement took a month to complete. It was decided that Freddie would belong to Miss Lucretia and that he'd go back to Baltimore to live. During his stay at the Wye River Place, he had noted that Aunt Jenny and Uncle Noah were still missing. And he also learned that his mother had died. His memory of her visit with the ginger cake he would cherish the rest of his life.

Chapter 6

When Fred (he outgrew the name Freddie) was about 14 years old, his hunger for learning was almost overpowering. Recalling his feeling of being "divided up" as part of Captain Anthony's property, he determined that one day he'd be free. He vowed he would not be regarded as another person's possession.

Hugh decided the lad should spend more time at the shipyard, learning to work there now that Tommy was more independent. "We'll make a caulker out of you one of these days," he prophesied.

Fred already knew what the caulking trade involved, for he had watched the tradesmen at work, pounding oakum into the seams of ships, then covering the seams with melted pitch, which prevented them from leaking.

He hurried through Miss Sophia's chores and errands to be free to go to the waterfront and its excitement. There he maintained the fires burning under the steam box used to heat and bend timbers to specific shapes for the carpenters to use. And he kept general watch over the shipyard.

Whenever he had the chance, Fred would

secretly earn money shining shoes. And one day he proudly put his money on a bookshop counter and announced, "I'd like to buy a *Columbian Orator*, please."

The clerk stared at him. "I'll declare! Why, you can't read a word."

Fred hid the book between his loft wall and a sea chest. Done during snatched moments, his reading of it became a gigantic labor, but he sorted out the words and sentences sufficiently to discuss the material with his two white friends, William and Henry.

In the book Fred found a conversation between a master and his runaway slave, the slave pointing out so well his views on slavery that he received his freedom. Fred was exultant. He'd been able to read a message from his book—one especially for himself!

Abolitionist—Fred heard the word often now. It caused heated discussions and arguments and quarrels among friends visiting the Aulds and on the wharves.

An angry slave was claimed to have killed his master, and Hugh said positively that the abolitionists were behind that. Another slave was accused of setting a house on fire, and again Hugh announced that abolitionists had influenced the man. Although now able to consult the Aulds' dictionary, Fred still did not know who the abolitionists were, for the dictionary only said, "Abolition: the act of abolishing."

Then his friends from Philpot Street helped by lending him a newspaper in which he found reference to petitions from the North for the abolition of slavery in the District of Columbia, and for the slave trade between the States to end.

At last he found his answer. Abolitionists were people working to put an end to slavery!

One day he helped two Irishmen unload some rock. One of them asked, "Are you a slave, lad?"

Fred nodded.

The man turned to his companion. "Such a shame," he remarked, "for such a nice-looking, strong, and promising lad to be owned by another!"

"Run away, my boy!" the other advised. "Run to the North. That's what the likes of you do when they're tired of not being free to be their own selves. You'd find friends up there. They'd help you."

Afraid to believe in their sincerity, Fred made no response. He had heard that some encouraged slaves to escape and then captured them to return them to their masters to gain the reward money. But their words remained with him.

A minister named Hanson met the youth on the street one day. "Do you love the Lord, lad?" he asked.

"I don't know," Fred stammered. Then he added, "If the Lord loved me, would I be a slave? Or would I be free and happy?"

Pastor Hanson replied thoughtfully, "Did you ever think that perhaps you could be free and happy *inside yourself* even though you are a slave? Jesus can do that for you, and if you'd allow Him, He could use you to help bring an end to slavery. Have you ever thought that God might be waiting for you to be His special worker for your people?" He put his arm about Fred's shoulders. "You think about what I have said, lad. And remember, no matter what happens, the Lord Jesus does love you."

There followed a period of churning thoughts and emotions in Fred. Urges to move the world welled up in him. Yes, he must do something, *anything*, to better the situation of all slaves. He recalled now how lighthearted he'd felt when he'd set out on the *Sally Lloyd* to live in Baltimore, and he supposed he'd never feel so carefree again. "Dear Lord," he'd often cry, "teach me what I must do and how I must do it. I'm here waiting for You to show me the way."

At Pastor Hanson's church he met Charles Johnson, a kindly black man who seemed to sense Fred's needs. Johnson taught him how to pray and what for. The youth began to believe that God was answering his prayers by sending people to him who would shape his life and help him understand both himself and God.

And then Uncle Lawson entered his life. Fred first noticed the old man driving a dray filled with goods through the Baltimore streets. For some unknown reason he particularly attracted Fred, and he followed the freight wagon.

When Uncle Lawson stopped to make a delivery, he prayed. Fred smiled to himself. A deliveryman doffing his cap and praying in a dray!

Several times he followed the dray and saw that Uncle Lawson was indeed a praying man. Introducing himself to the old fellow, he soon discovered their friendship growing. Uncle Lawson led Fred to give his heart to Christ.

One day on a muddy street the young man found a trampled Bible. Carrying it home, he secretly washed and dried it and began reading it. Now he would not have to steal bits of reading from the Aulds' Bible during their absence.

Fred became deeply attached to Uncle Lawson, attending prayer meetings and spending his leisure time with him. The man could read a little, and Fred helped him improve. Sometimes they sang and prayed together. The Aulds did not interfere with his association with Uncle Lawson, but one day Hugh saw Fred leave a meeting at the home of free black people and forbade him to attend again.

Uncle Lawson and Fred often discussed what future lay ahead for the youth. "God has a big work for you to do, lad," the man said, and then added, "Never be bitter about having been born a slave. Bitterness and hate are like a fire that will eat away at your soul until you're of no use in the world. But when your heart's filled with love, then the good Lord can use you to work for Him. And look at things this way, Fred: The fact that you were born a slave puts you in a position to speak out against slavery, since you know what you're talking about."

Searching for some way he might begin to help his people, Fred started a school for young black boys. He'd teach them what he knew of reading and writing and God.

Sometimes he'd put his thoughts and emotions on paper, then read them to Uncle Lawson, who would chuckle with delight and pride at his young friend's growth. "I knew! I always knew, Fred Bailey, that you were clever! You must let God have your cleverness, and everything will be all right," he'd say, patting the youth's shoulders.

RAINBOWS OF PROMISE

In March, 1833, when Fred Bailey was 16 years old, Hugh roused him one morning before dawn. "You're going to live with my brother, Master Thomas," he said. "Step lively and get down there to the *Amanda* at Smith's Wharf."

Fred shrank back in horror from his master. Auld had made the announcement as if it were no more than "Go down to the shipyard and get me some rope." The man could casually and callously change his slave's life without allowing him even a farewell to Sophia and Tommy. He'd heard the two brothers quarreling in the night, and apparently Thomas had demanded to take Fred to serve him.

He raced to Uncle Lawson's lodgings, where he found his friend already preparing for the day's work. They embraced, clinging to each other in a despairing way. Uncle Lawson is the closest to a father I have ever known, the slave boy thought. What shall I do without him?

"Always remember," the old man told him, "there's something special the good Lord has in mind for you."

"How I'll miss him and my other friends!" Fred lamented as he ran toward the dock. "And who'll teach in my boys' school now? Is God letting me be snatched away just as I'm getting educated to do something?"

Sudden flashes of something he'd seen the day before made a leaden dullness in his chest. He'd been roaming the wharves in late afternoon, enjoying as usual the waterfront activity, when his pleasure died, for he'd seen black men and women and children chained together and boarding a ship.

"Where's she bound?" he asked a young sailor

going aboard the vessel.

"New Orleans," the crewman replied. "Make yourself scarce, boy, or they'll likely run you aboard, a nice-looking lad like you."

The scene lay heavily on his heart. "Dear Lord," he prayed again, "help me find a way to do something for myself and my people!"

As the *Amanda* took him to St. Michaels, a fishing village on the Chesapeake Bay some forty miles from Baltimore, he learned that Miss Lucretia and her brother Master Andrew had died of cholera since the dividing up of the estate, and that Thomas had married again. The new Mrs. Auld and little Amanda, a miniature of her mother, Lucretia, were waiting at the dock to meet the sloop.

When he reached the Thomas Auld farm, he found there his Aunt Priscilla, his sister Eliza, and Henney, a girl cousin. And once again his insides gnawed from hunger as they had in the lean times at Aunt Katy's kitchen. Thomas Auld would throw wasted food to the dogs, while at the same time he let his servants go hungry.

Should he steal food or beg as the other servants did? Or should he die from hunger? His conscience pulled him one way and another, as did also his physical agonies.

Life had been a mistake, Fred thought. He didn't belong to Thomas and his new wife, Rowena, but to Miss Lucretia. For that reason he could not and would not call Thomas "Master." It was not the truth as he saw it. The man was simply *Captain* Auld, and that he would remain. Unfortunately, Auld did not see things the same way he did. When Fred voiced his convictions to the man, he infuriated his would-be master. But Thomas was not the only one who got upset. His wife listened silently, her face turning red. Then Rowena announced, biting each word off, "We have a troublemaker on our hands, husband; my woman sense tells me."

Chapter 7

"That's not woman sense," her husband replied, "for I also sense trouble ahead. But there's always Covey to remedy the situation."

She laughed. "So Edward Covey really does attend to the rebellious ones?"

"An understatement, Mrs. Auld," he responded.

Fred felt plunged into deepest gloom. Opportunities for self-improvement such as he'd had in Baltimore no longer existed. I have slid backward many steps, he thought, when all I seem to think about is food.

Each morning as he filled the huge woodbox in the kitchen, Fred heard the Aulds at breakfast. "Merciful God," the man would pray, "bless our household in basket and in store, and save us at last in Thy eternal kingdom."

Fred thought about that prayer. Was Thomas Auld's God the same as his? The God whom Uncle Lawson loved? Did He send Thomas plenty of food and yet permit his servants to go hungry?

August, and the air seemed vibrant with camp meeting fever and summer heat. The Methodists were assembling about eight miles from the Auld home, and their meetings would continue a week. Worshipers swarmed to the site, even two steamboats full of them from Baltimore.

Fred slipped away to see for himself what all the fuss was about, and found a circle of dwelling tents surrounding the giant assembly tent. A second circle of tents surrounded the others, and on the outside, covered wagons, carts, carriages, and surreys also served as makeshift homes. On the outskirts of this temporary village glowed campfires, from which floated pleasant smells of cooking food. Laughter, talk, and singing filled the air.

Thomas ordered his servants to attend the meetings. Perhaps, Fred wondered, had the man sensed that he had been thinking about disappearing while the family attended them? An air of expectancy hung over the arriving worshipers. Flaring pine knots lighted the meeting tent, and one heard on every hand the steady tramp of feet, the rustle of voluminous skirts, the greeting of friends.

An altar stood in front of the pulpit, and straw covered the floor of the enclosure that the people referred to as "the mourners' place." Behind the pulpit and to the left was a place designated for black worshipers.

Fred remained alert throughout the meeting. Once during the sermon the preacher spoke directly to "those over to the left." At the close of the meeting Fred counted one hundred people in the mourners' enclosure who professed sorrow for their past sins. It dismayed him that the mourners' area was out of bounds for black worshipers. Would there always be one place for blacks and another for whites? Even in heaven?

Going to sleep that night, he remembered a song that the congregation had sung:

Come, saints and sinners, hear me tell
 The wonders of Emmanuel,
Who saved me from a burning hell
And taught my soul with Him to dwell,
And gave me heavenly union.

He recalled that attendants had passed among the white people sheets of paper containing the words of the various spiritual songs. But "those over to the left" had to learn the words from the others. The camp meeting leaders seemed to assume that no one among the slaves was capable of reading. Fred wondered what he would have done had someone offered him a page by mistake. Would he have revealed that he could read?

One night the Aulds "went forward," and Fred thought to himself, Now that Thomas and Rowena Auld profess to love Jesus truly, they'll give us our freedom. And at the very least they'll see we are never hungry again. But though the Aulds entertained the visiting ministers with their very best, nothing changed in the servants' diet. One of the ministers did show his concern for the servants, though, and talked to slaveholders in the area about working toward freeing their slaves.

A young man, James Mitchell, invited Fred to help start a school for a group of boys. Delightedly Fred helped collect spelling books and New Testaments, and the first day they had twenty students.

Happiness from doing something worthwhile began to fill the empty, lonely places in his life. But just as Hugh had destroyed Sophia's best efforts to help him read, so Thomas and two of his neighbors put an end to the new school. They beat the teachers and forbade further lessons.

Another episode also disturbed Fred. For an alleged wrongdoing, Thomas tied up Fred's cousin Henney and whipped her. She was still smarting from the lashes when the slaveowner read to her from Luke 12:47: "That servant, which knew his lord's will, and prepared not himself, neither did according to his will, shall be beaten with many stripes."

I should have had my senses about me and taken her punishment for her, Fred thought too late, and his conscience troubled him miserably.

Her hands almost completely disabled by a scalding accident, Henney was unable to do the chores the Aulds expected of her. Irritated about her handicap, Thomas sent her to his sister, who also found the girl a burden and returned her. Unwilling to keep a slave who could not work, Auld sent her away. His lack of mercy troubled Fred greatly, and he felt that he would choke from the frustration of not being able to do anything to comfort his cousin.

One day a horse belonging to Thomas Auld broke loose and headed for his father-in-law's farm. Thomas dispatched Fred to retrieve the animal. Aunt Mary, the cook there, received him warmly, and after commenting on his thinness, fed him well. From then on, the horse managed to run off with regularity, Fred was not nearly so hungry, and he made a wonderful friend of Aunt Mary.

Winter's chill brought its depression and bitterness. In fact, except for Aunt Mary, Fred could find absolutely no cheer in life. "Are You there, God?" he asked on more than one occasion. Sometimes he wondered whether God had forgotten that he was here. That he had offered himself to Him to work for his people and that his present situation tied him hand and foot.

In the cold darkness of November 12-13, 1833, Fred stirred from an uneasy sleep. Dogs were barking, it seemed, all across the length and breadth of Maryland, and he was sure he heard a woman's screams. He sprang to the door of his cabin and, looking out, saw the sky ablaze with shooting stars. At first he was terrified, then he ran outdoors, his face to the sky and the chafing wind, and held his arms toward heaven.

"The Lord Jesus is coming!" he exclaimed, and began to laugh. "Aunt Priscilla, Eliza! Come quickly! It's the end of the world! The Lord Jesus will appear at any time." The women came running, clutching their flimsy clothing about them as they tried to protect themselves from the cold, and the Aulds stood clinging to each other.

The Lord Jesus was coming!

A great joy flooded Fred. No more slavery. No more hunger. New hands for Henney. He'd read of and heard about the end of the world many times. Now he need worry no more about working to set his black brothers and sisters free. Jesus' coming would liberate them forever!

But daylight brought life's routines and chores and unfulfilled longings back. The world hadn't ended, and Jesus had not returned to claim His children.

In early December, Thomas Auld told him, "I've had you nine months, and you've done me no good. I'm tired of hoping for a change in you. On hiring day you go to work for Covey. He'll make you take notice!"

Aunt Mary had warned Fred about Edward Covey. He managed to eke out a living on his rented farm by taking unwilling slaves to break them. Covey had the reputation of being one of the most effective slave breakers in all of Maryland.

On a chill, dreary January 1, 1834, the wind slapping at him, Fred trudged alone to the Covey farm. Recalling the catch in the nets that Grandma Betsy had brought in, he felt as trapped as those fish.

"I'll never be able to do anything while I belong to another man," he said aloud.

Terror struck him as he listened to Edward Covey's directions for handling the oxen to bring in a load of firewood that he must get from the woods about two miles from the Covey house. "Dear Lord Jesus, get me through this job," he prayed as soon as the man left.

The animals pulled reasonably well until they passed through the field gate; then they headed in a galloping frenzy toward the woods. They dragged the cart over huge stumps and slammed it against tree trunks. Fred yelled all the words Mr. Covey had directed, but they had no influence over the beasts. He tugged on the lead ropes, but the oxen kept up their rampage until he feared they would throw him from the cart and crush him between it and a tree trunk.

"Dear God, put Your hand on the beasts," he

cried. Then over tumbled the cart, and the oxen entangled themselves in a sapling grove. Praying as he worked, Fred managed to reassemble the cart's scattered parts; then he cut away the saplings and freed the animals. Seeing they were subdued now, he loaded as much wood as possible on the cart in the hope that the heavy load would keep them under control. He hoped that his first strenuous efforts would please Covey.

All went well until Fred opened the heavy yard gate. The sound of it dragging on the ground sent both oxen bellowing and plunging through the opening, catching the gate between a wheel and the body of the cart. The gate splintered, and Fred came within inches of getting crushed to death.

Shaken, Fred still hoped that in spite of the gate catastrophe, Mr. Covey would be satisified with his work. But no.

"Clumsy idiot! Can't you do anything properly?" the man hissed. "Get back for another load of wood, and don't take so long!"

On that second trip Edward Covey ordered a halt. Rushing upon Fred and ripping away his worn shirt, he whipped him angrily until he could continue no longer. "That will teach you not to ruin gates!" he snarled when he at last regained his breath.

That first day set the tone of Fred's next six months. He would receive nothing save cruelty, no matter how hard he worked. And all the while he cried in his heart for the dreams he'd had in Baltimore. They now seemed to have vanished forever, replaced by constant scheming as to how he could escape in such open country.

One summer day Fred, with Eli, a hired-out slave, and Mr. Covey's regular men, worked in the "treading yard" where horses trod wheat from its husks. In a rush to get the job done Fred collapsed from dizziness.

"I heard the fan stop!" Edward shrieked. The fan separated the chaff from the wheat. "So you're the trouble!" he accused when he saw the teen-ager lying in the shade. "Lazy and dishonest!"

"Mr. Covey, I was dizzy from the heat and I——"

"You cheat!" he exploded, kicking the slave in the ribs. "Get up this minute!"

Fred struggled to his feet, but fell when he tried to pick up his tub. "I can't," he gasped.

"*Can't* isn't a word around here!" the slave breaker shouted. Grabbing a chunk of wood, he slammed it down against Fred's head. The young man lay panting, blood running down his face.

Chapter 8

Fred watched the cruel man walk toward his house. I've had enough, he thought. If I stay here I'll be killed.

He lay waiting, praying for strength to return. What would Uncle Lawson say if he could see him now? Would he still insist there was no room for bitterness? No rainbows brightened this darkest of hours.

Inch by searing inch he crawled a good way toward the woods before Covey discovered his movements. "Get back here!" he yelled from the house.

Summoning all the strength he possibly could, Fred ran and stumbled toward the shelter of the woods. When he reached the Aulds' house, his owners appeared genuinely shocked at the sight of him—dusty, blood caked, and in a state of collapse. As Rowena tended his wounds, Fred heard her husband pacing the floor. He will take me back, the youth thought. Anything is better than being under the power of Edward Covey!

But Thomas stopped and turned to the injured slave. "Well, Fred Bailey, what do you want *me* to do? What do you suggest?" Then his anger took charge of him. "I'll tell you what's to be done. You're going back to Covey!"

Fred stumbled in disbelief toward the door.

"Wait!" Auld called. "You may stay here tonight, but you leave at daybreak."

That night Fred lay awake, feeling lonely and weak and thinking that not a person knew or cared about his dilemma. "God, are You *really* there?" he moaned. "I want to believe. Help me believe that You see me—and care."

Edward Covey awaited his return the next morning with a rope and a cowhide, anger blanching his face. At the sight of him Fred rushed back through the cornfields and the safety of the woods.

All day he hid without any food or anything to drink, his head aching furiously. At dusk as he was making a leaf bed, he heard footsteps. His heart hammering, his mouth dry, he hid behind a giant tree.

Then he saw Sandy, a slave he knew, who was on his way home to spend his day of rest with his wife, who was a freedwoman.

"Look at you, Fred!" Sandy whispered. "What has happened?"

Quickly Fred told his miserable story. "You must come home with me," the other slave said. "You need care."

Fred hesitated. "I can't, Sandy," he replied. "You'll get thirty-nine lashes of the stoutest whip if you're found sheltering me."

"Come on, now, and be quiet about it."

When they reached the cabin at midnight, Millie, Sandy's wife, arose to cook some Indian meal mush and an ashcake for each of the men. And while they waited for the food to be ready she dressed Fred's injured head.

"I'm sorry to be a trouble," Fred apologized, "and I'm doubly sorry to be placing you in danger."

"Nonsense!" they said in unison, and Millie added. "It is the good Lord's work, giving bread to the hungry and comfort to a brother." By the torchlight Fred saw the compassion reflected in her eyes. It is through God's true children, Fred nodded to himself that we learn most about His love for us.

"Why does everything go wrong for me?" he asked abruptly.

"If you're asking me," Sandy responded. "Tom Auld is afraid of you. You can read and write, so naturally he and all the local slaveholders fear you. You could write passes for yourself and all the others for miles around, so, of course, they want to push you down and make you feel you're always in the wrong, to break your spirit."

"Where I am at Covey's, on that exposed land, anybody could see me if I tried to run away," Fred said wearily.

Sandy took pieces of root from a shelf, saying, "Carry this, Fred. Go on back to Covey, and nothing bad will happen to you. If you don't return to him, you're likely to be sold to the South. The root has special charms, and it will make things come out all right."

Grateful for the kindness shown him, Fred took the pieces of root to please Sandy.

Strange, he thought, that when he returned, Edward Covey was civil to him. Surely the root has no magic charm!

Long before dawn on Monday, Edward Covey sent Fred to feed and curry the horses and then to get equipment out of the stable loft for the day's work. As Fred began his ascent to the loft, Covey grabbed his legs and tried to tie them.

That's when rebellion took possession of Fred. He had put forth his best efforts for Edward Covey, and he saw now that his best would never be sufficient. No longer could he submit to such cruelty and cowardice. For the first time he saw himself as weak for having put up with such teatment for so long.

I'm young and I'm strong, he thought, but I'll be of no use to anyone if I allow my body to be ruined. Seizing Covey's cord and throwing it aside, he sprang upon his persecutor, and after a long fight, pinned him to the ground.

"Drag him away!" Covey ordered, but his farmworkers appeared not to hear his plea. They also had suffered from his cruelty. Two hours later Fred let the man loose and arose, trembling from his great effort.

Day after day he expected reprisal, but Edward Covey made no move. Gone was Fred's lack of ambition, his caring-about-nothing mood. Once again he longed to learn and to do God's work for his fellow slaves.

But in reflective moments he was sorry he had felt forced to pay Edward Covey "in kind." "He could have sent you for a public whipping for what you did to him," one of the farmhands told Fred, "but he has a great slave-breaker reputation to keep."

Early Christmas morning, 1834, Fred headed

once more toward the Thomas Auld household. But broken by Edward Covey, as Thomas had intended? Not at all. With a firm belief that the future would bring good things, he walked along proudly and confidently.

He was "hired out" next to the Freeland farm for a two-year period, and Mr. Freeland, although expecting a strenuous day's work, proved to be a kind and generous master. Good food and long nights of rest renewed the strength Fred had lost at the Aulds and at the Covey farm.

Soon he started a school for fellow farmworkers and any others who wished to attend. A freedman offered the use of his home as a classroom for the forty students. Uncle Lawson would be happy if he could know of his success, Fred thought. He wished the old man were still alive so he could step into his classroom and see what the youth was accomplishing.

His knowing that he was in constant peril of discovery, however, dampened his pleasure—but not his vision of what he could do with words and ideas and an attitude of caring about his students.

With the passing of the months, Fred began to plant thoughts and plans of escape in the minds of other slaves on the farm. Although again he heard the all-too-familiar arguments and warnings against escape, he paid no heed to them, but wrote "passes" for himself and the others who wished to flee with him.

The day before the appointed date, Sandy, who also worked at Freeland's farm, said he'd had warning dreams. They told that escape meant certain death, but Fred and his five companions held to their plans.

Breakfast had scarcely begun when a neighbor, Mr. Hamilton, and several law officers came galloping on horses to the Freeland home.

"We're looking for Fred Bailey," one of the men said. "It's claimed he's been in some mischief in town. We must take him in to be examined."

Fred stared at his accusers. He had not been away from the farm, but what could be gained by arguing with them? Hamilton turned to one of the officers. "Constable, don't you think we should search these young men for passes that have supposedly been written by me?"

Now Fred guessed that Sandy had betrayed him, because he'd been the only one who'd refused to join the escapees. A picture of Sandy's wife floated before his eyes, and he could well understand why the slave preferred to stay where he could spend each weekend with her. And was it his superstition about his bad dreams that had led him to betray his friends? Did he actually feel he was being kind by preventing their flight?

As the men began searching for the passes, Fred was glad that they had gotten rid of all of them before the party had dismounted. But the law officers still led him and the others away.

The sheriff summoned Thomas Auld to the Easton jail.

"What have I done?" Fred asked him. "What charge or evidence has been brought before us?"

Thomas shrugged. "Well, what *have you done?*"

In spite of no charge or evidence, all of the young men remained in jail. The others were released the next day, but Fred had to stay and endure the taunting of would-be slave buyers, who visited him frequently. They made a mockery of examining him and putting a price on him. Then one of them lifted the back of Fred's shirt and drew in his breath. "I'll declare, this is Covey's work!" he exclaimed in apparent shock. "Whip stripes every which way, and one on top of the other! I've heard that Covey tried to break this one but lost his reputation on him."

After a week Thomas Auld appeared again at the jail with the news that a friend would take Fred "to the South," where he'd work for eight years. Released into Auld's custody, Fred returned home to prepare for the long trip, but within a few days Thomas told him he was sending him back to Baltimore for his "own safety's sake. The farmers in these parts have warned me they won't tolerate a troublemaker who can read and write associating with their slaves. If you'll settle down and work hard, behaving yourself, I'll give you your freedom when you're 25."

Fred returned to the Baltimore Aulds and went to work as a caulking apprentice in William Gardner's shipyard. The tradesmen there were working on orders for two naval vessels that they had to complete quickly. But it soon became evident to Fred that it could be a long time before he would become a skilled caulker, for the shipwrights continually called on him to do small tasks for them.

At home and at the shipyards, discussion about the abolition of slavery had grown more intense than it had been even before Fred had left for St.

Michaels. He heard conversations about the forming of an antislavery society and the mention of certain leaders, including William Lloyd Garrison and William Wells Brown. And some claimed that England would soon abolish slavery.

Increasingly alert, Fred secretly labored over books and newspapers when he had an opportunity. He heard slaveholders discuss the problems the northern States had created for them, and again he heard of petitions before Congress to end slavery.

Loneliness for Uncle Lawson marred his days. No one, he was sure, would ever be able to take the man's place in his affections.

Chapter

9

Fred Bailey sought out his Baltimore associates of earlier times, his free friends, who made it possible for him to attend some of their meetings. And assistance came to him through his connection with the East Baltimore Mutual Improvement Society and the Society of Friends. Individuals in both groups helped young blacks receive an education, and Fred was one who gained greatly from their activities.

Free blacks now attended ten churches in Baltimore. They had members who saved money toward the purchase of land, horses, and conveyances for newly freed blacks to use. Their dedication and love touched Fred's heart, as they did their part to better their people in the spirit that Jesus had taught His followers. Like Uncle Lawson, Pastor Hanson, and Charles Johnson, they placed themselves in God's hands for Him to use to answer the prayers of the needy. "I must learn to do as they do," Fred told himself.

The first few months after his return from St. Michaels, Fred felt restless. The experiences he'd had on the Eastern Shore, his own longings for freedom, his urgency to do his part to help it come to all slaves, and his feeling that he must somehow escape, but not sure how, kept him in turmoil.

At night when he tried to sleep, he would think of Edward Covey. What made Covey the cruel, angry person he had become? Was he the kind of individual Uncle Lawson had meant when he spoke of bitterness destroying the one who harbored it in his heart? And if so, what was the acid that ate away at him?

Dear Uncle Lawson, the young man thought. I'm sure he must have suffered many things over the years, and perhaps he had many causes for bitterness, but instead he possessed understanding.

Comparing the lives of Uncle Lawson and Edward Covey in his mind, Fred began to realize what Jesus had come to teach: that love is good, and that hate and cruelty are evil.

Remembering Henney, he thought of how he might have taken her punishment for her, and it led him to see more clearly that Someone *had* taken *his* punishment for him. "He was bruised for our iniquities," Fred thought.

And he relived his imprisonment at the Easton jail. What if those men had had the power to do more than taunt him? What kind of experiences would he have endured? And what had it meant for those many who had, indeed, been sold?

Over and over in Fred's mind there tumbled thoughts of the injustice of slavery. Of the frustration of not being allowed to be the person you longed to be, of not being able to grow and to do, of not being permitted to reach your full promise as a man or woman.

Suddenly a great thankfulness for the ordeals of his Eastern Shore experience came to him. They had shown him what he didn't want the remainder of his life to be, and he could see he would never be able to do the things he really wanted to do unless he gained his freedom. Risks there would be—great ones. But he must take them. To wait until he was 25 years old was not good enough. By that time Thomas Auld could change his mind, especially since by then he'd be a skilled tradesman and would therefore be a profitable slave.

One night Hugh waited for him to return home. "Where have you been?"

"At prayer meeting."

"Stupid nonsense! You don't go there again, Fred Bailey. Won't it ever get through your head that mixing with those people gives you big ideas that aren't true? All men are *not* to be treated in the same manner. Get it through your head that you're a common slave, and will be for the rest of your life! And mind you, I'll flog you soundly if I catch you attending another such meeting."

The threat did not trouble him. And he was glad he knew that Hugh Auld was mistaken. He was not common, but a child of God with a most uncommon work to do.

Trouble broke out on the wharves. Disputes arose over the poor wages given white laborers, because employers could pay much less to readily available slaves. And in some cases slaves received no pay. As a result, whites sought to keep slaves out of their trades. Some demanded the dismissal of all blacks.

Angry groups attacked Fred several times, until

he dreaded the arrival of each new day. One day four men beat him cruelly, leaving him severely wounded.

"We must act, Hugh Auld," Sophia said, a new tone of command in her voice. "Whatever the grievances, this could have meant Fred's death. Things are completely out of hand. We must do something!"

As she bathed his head wounds with wonderful gentleness, Fred remembered that others had done the same thing for him—Lucretia Auld, and more recently Sandy's wife, Millie, and even Rowena Auld. Then as Sophia brought the dressing for his wounds, their eyes met and held. His heart beat with gladness, for he saw written there in her gaze that old expression, the one he had seen when he was a small child. It contained affection, hope, concern, and ambition for him. But added to all those now was the same expression he'd seen in the luminous eyes of Millie—compassion. And it seemed to Fred that Sophia Auld was trying to say in that brief exchange, "I suffer because I did not follow my true feelings to do what I should have done when you were a little fellow. Please try to understand!"

Fred knew that that moment would live on forever in his heart. And he thought he understood, for there was little difference in their circumstances. Sophia Auld had also been, and still was, like a slave. The habits of thinking, customs, and the prejudices of others had bound hor. Sho had not been true to herself. Someone else had denied her the privilege of doing what her heart urged her to do. How well I understand, he thought. And the difference between their circumstances now, he mused, was that Sophia's opportunity was gone, but he was young, with life still stretching out in invitation before him.

As soon as Fred was physically able, Hugh took him to see a magistrate, who, shrugging, asked, "What can I do? Do you have a white witness to these acts?"

At home Hugh said, "We won't be sending Fred back to Gardner's, Sophia. Take good care of him until he feels well, and then we'll decide what we should do for him."

Hugh, having failed in his own shipyard business during Fred's absence from Baltimore, had become a foreman in the Price shipyard. He took Fred there to complete his caulking apprenticeship. On his new job the youth found fellow workers who willingly shared their knowledge of ciphering with him.

At the East Baltimore Mutual Improvement Society, which freed blacks invited him to join—an unheard-of honor—he kept adding to his knowledge of the Bible, English, history, geography, and public speaking. And there he also took a lively part in discussions and debates.

Anna Murray came into his life at those meetings. Born of slave parents at Denton, not far from where Fred had lived at Tuckahoe, she was free and in service in a home in Baltimore. She and Fred learned to love each other, which intensified his determination to make his bid for freedom. He did not intend to bring upon her the suffering she would endure should he continue to belong to another man. In fact, Thomas Auld would probably not permit him to marry her. And in the future they would have their children to think about. Fred refused to pass on to them a heritage of slavery. Free, he could be a *man*, the head of his family. The idea of taking home his earnings to a wife and children he loved, instead of to a master, thrilled him.

In quiet ways Fred tried to gain from his Improvement Society friends support for his escape plans, but they said they must confine their interests to their educational activities. However, members of the society told him about the Vigilance Committee in New York, which tried to protect blacks in the city from being molested, kidnapped and sold back into slavery.

Fred earned good wages now. Hugh seemed pleased with his efforts.

One evening, leaving the shipyard, he discovered he'd lost his week's pay. What could he say to Hugh? The man would be angry and suspicious, and would accuse him of having spent the money or of holding it back.

Retracing his footsteps, searching in every possible place the money might have fallen, he met a seaman he'd known since his days at Gardner's shipyard. "A disaster, Stanley," he greeted his friend. "I've lost my pay. Hugh Auld will be furious when I tell him."

The sailor fished in his pocket and then held out his hand. "Does this look familiar?"

It was his pay envelope, and all in order! "How can I thank you!"

"Don't try," his friend said with a grin. "I heard a good man say once that doing the right thing is reward in itself." Then he grew serious. "Fred, why don't you leave here? There's something better a person like you could be doing with his life than working to take home his pay to a master for the rest of his days. You know that, don't you?"

The man's lecture burned in Fred's mind as he hurried home, and suddenly he had an idea. Stanley! A friend. Trustworthy. A seaman. Fred had heard that some slaves had escaped disguised as seamen. Perhaps the same plan would work for him. But, of course, Stanley must have a say in that. He'd be putting his friend in peril if the idea became reality. Since Fred would be asking a great deal, he'd need to give the subject much more thought.

Thomas Auld arrived in Baltimore in the spring of 1838, and Fred took the opportunity to make a request that had been much on his mind. He asked his owner to allow him to find his own work contracts instead of staying at the one shipyard for a weekly wage.

"Definitely not!" Thomas decided. "You'd be scheming to break away. I'd be playing into your hands, giving you so much freedom. No, we've been through your escape tries before. Not again. And let me tell you, young man, if you *do* disappear at any time, I'll find you, even if I have to turn the world inside out. Now, no more of this. And not a word to my brother about this conversation."

A few weeks later, however, Fred did bring the matter to Hugh. "I'm sure I could double my earnings," he said.

Hugh consented. "Of course, there'll be conditions to be met," he warned. "You'll find your own work and collect your own pay. Each week you'll bring home three dollars to me and you'll pay Miss Sophia room and board. Finally, you'll buy your own clothing and your own tools. If you fail in any way, back you go to a weekly wage. And not a word to Thomas about this," he added, "or he'll be demanding extra money from you."

Chapter 10

Employment was uncertain and irregular, and Fred Bailey would need to earn six dollars each week to meet his obligations to the Aulds. But he felt the benefits were worth the pressures. Bargaining for jobs, handling money, and being able to make choices gave him a buoyant sense of freedom.

Also, he could spend more time with Anna and his free friends, and he could secretly contact Stanley for advice and help in his plans to disappear from Baltimore.

One evening at twilight the two hid behind a pile of newly stacked lumber at the site of Fred's latest job.

"I know I'm asking far too much, Stanley," Fred ventured, "but would you consider helping me get away?"

"Away? You mean escape?" Stanley asked, his voice sounding tense.

"Yes, escape, disguised as a seaman in your clothes."

"What about papers?" asked Stanley. "My seaman's papers say I'm black-skinned. Your skin is kind of bronze. If you traveled by train, someone would compare you with your papers, and the description would have to be the same as you appear."

"I could write a pass for myself and not bother about your protection," Fred suggested. "That would also take care of your being without it if someone might ask for your identification."

"No, that wouldn't do," Stanley replied. "If you're traveling as a seaman you must have that protection with you to prove you're not a slave."

"You mean you'd run the risk of being without your documents in order to let me carry them."

His friend nodded. "I meant it when I said there is something better you could be doing than turning over your pay to your master for the rest of your life. So I'm willing to run risks to back up my words."

Fred put his arm around the man's shoulders. "You put me to shame," he said. "I doubt that I could make such a sacrifice for a friend."

"I'll be at my lodgings tomorrow. Come over and try on my clothes and look at my protection."

He had to make additional plans. For example, he would eventually have to return the seaman's outfit to Stanley. Then he'd need his own "free" papers. Studying Anna's document, he prepared a similar one for himself.

Also, he had a conference with Anna. "To avoid the ticket agent's comparing you with a protection description," she said, "I'll buy a railroad ticket for you. If you'll plan to arrive on the platform when the train is almost due to pull away, I'll be standing at the door of the last car, the car for blacks, to give you your ticket." Then she added, "Fred, once you leave, it's possible we'll never meet again."

"I know that," he replied.

She sighed. "There are some things in this life that simply must be done," she said, "and I know that this happens to be one of them."

Anna smiled then—that calm smile he loved. Taking his hands in hers, she kissed him on each cheek. "Smile, Fred," she said softly. "I'll see you in New York by mid-September."

Fred had thought about all the things that could happen to him on the long trip from Baltimore to New York, and he had often favored simply walking away one day toward the North, sure that he could outwit the kidnappers that supposedly frequented every northward road. But now Anna was his big concern. If he attempted to escape by foot, it might be months before he could send word for her to join him. And though going by train had added risks of discovery, he'd reach New York by the second day of his flight and would be able to send word back to her almost immediately.

His friend Isaac Rhodes promised to see that his belongings arrived in good order at the train. He'd run along the platform and throw Fred's canvas bag through a window that the fugitive would keep open in the last car. The train would probably be moving by then, and Issac would need to toss it on the train quickly.

At home Fred tried to appear calm, but it seemed to him his plans must be printed in large words all over him and that the Aulds could not possibly fail to read them. He was glad that Tommy, who surely would have noticed his uneasy mood, was now away at sea.

Daily he overheard conversations about the

Mirror of Liberty, the first black magazine, produced by David Ruggles; about Freedman Charles Redmond and his antislavery lecture tours; and Joshua Geddings, the first abolitionist to head for Congress.

Someday they may be talking about me in this same way, Fred thought. The Lord is the only one who knows what I'll be doing, and I know He'll help me in whatever I'm called to do.

That week Fred worked extra hard. He'd saved a little from each pay, but he needed every penny it was possible for him to earn until he could find work in the North. The last night of one week he had to work late to finish the job he'd promised he would complete that day. Earlier he'd arranged to meet some of his young friends to travel in a dray to a camp meeting held about twelve miles from Baltimore. Since he'd already kept them waiting, he decided that he could not take the time to go home to give the money to Master Hugh. When he returned home would be soon enough.

Arriving at the big tent, he thought about how long it had been since that other camp meeting on the Eastern Shore. At the sound of the hearty singing, memories came surging back. "'We have our trials here below,'" the worshipers sang enthusiastically, "'O Glory, Hallelujah! There's a better day a comin', Glory, Hallelujah!'"

Fred, fidgeting from the strain of waiting so many weeks, hoped that September 3 would be "a better day" for him.

For a moment he remembered Thomas and Rowena Auld at that other camp meeting; then suddenly his memories of his unhappiness with them seemed not to matter. Instead, he felt sorry for them. What you say and what you do must go hand in hand, he mused. If you say you have love in your heart, then you will show that love in your actions to everyone.

Fred snapped out of his reverie and his weariness when the preacher challenged in a loud voice, "Will you serve the Lord?"

Of course I'll serve the Lord, the young man thought. Why am I making such big and dangerous plans if I don't have that in mind?

When it came time to head back to Baltimore, his party could not find their horse. I should start for home on foot, Fred thought, to be back to work on time, but he remained to help search for the straying animal.

"All right!" Hugh shouted when Fred jumped off the dray cart and ran into the house. "You've proved yourself untrustworthy. No more hiring out!"

But in a few days Auld seemed to have second thoughts, for Fred had obligations to those for whom he'd contracted to do work. He worked harder than before, bringing home more pay than usual. Pleased, Hugh gave him back a portion.

As the day of escape neared, Fred's whole being churned inside. He had strong memories of his other attempts.

"Tomorrow!" he said to Anna.

"Yes, tomorrow. God be with us!"

"Tomorrow!" Fred told Isaac Rhodes.

"Yes, and may God will everything to be right for you, Fred."

"How will I thank you?" he said to Stanley

when he went to pick up the friend's seaman's papers.

"There's only one way you can thank me. You can get busy as soon as you're able and help free all men!"

The Aulds left for the evening, which gave Fred the opportunity needed to take the clothes to his room, where he carefully placed each item under his mattress: the red shirt, the tarpaulin hat, the trousers, and the tie.

That night as he removed them, the mattress rustled. A floorboard creaked, and Fred feared to breathe. Then as he went through the motions he had rehearsed in his mind, a torrent of thoughts rushed through his head. These clothes fit so well they were meant for me! But am I doing the right thing? Careful now. Easy down that ladder. Hugh Auld, you're snoring. Glad about that. There's a squeaky board near the door. Watch where I step. The latch. Very quietly, Fred Bailey. There! Now close the door softly. Be cautious. It will take only one person to see a black sailor rushing away from the Aulds, and the game will be up.

Stopping in the friendly shadows, he took off the sailor hat to make sure the hidden identity papers were securely in there, placed it back on at the correct angle again, and set off for the train, hoping his walk resembled a sailor's gait.

Although concentrating on persuading onlookers that he was not what he was—a runaway slave—a number of impressions still filtered through: coachmen's uniforms, dresses of silk, feathers on bonnets. Whips cracking, drivers shouting, and, even so early, the cry of a peanut vendor. The curtain rolled up on a coach window. Is that woman staring at me? Hurry, Fred Bailey!

The train engine snorted and puffed at the station. Someone yelled, "All aboard!"

Fred dashed for the last car. Then he spotted Anna—sedate, calm Anna. They embraced briefly. "A package for you. It's very valuable. Do take care not to lose it!" she placed it in his hand and closed his fingers tightly against it.

Not looking back, he rushed to a window of the crowded last car and pushed it open.

"What do you think you're doing!" the stout man in the window seat demanded. "My foot! You're crushing it, sailor."

The train lurched and began its caterpillar crawl. Then through the window the canvas bag came tumbling. Fred touched his not-yet-familiar hat and nodded to the man whose foot he'd hurt.

"I'm sorry I hurt you, sir," he said. "I was worried about my bag, but my friend got it here on time."

"So I see!" the offended man snarled.

The locomotive picked up speed. Gratefully Fred found an empty seat.

"Tickets and papers! Tickets and papers!" the conductor chanted. "Have them ready."

Now or never! The palms of his hands became sweaty, and his heart thumped madly. Taking the papers from the tarpaulin hat, he tried to think of a way of holding them that would not betray the shaking of his body.

"Now or never, Lord Jesus," he prayed. "Everything depends on now, and You know I can't stand the thought of my escape being never!"

"Well, sailor," the conductor greeted, "nice day to be on land."

"Yes, sir," Fred replied, handing over the documents.

"Let's see," the conductor said, scanning the description. "Yes—now, wait a minute . . ."

Chapter 11

"Now you stop that, Willie!" a woman snapped, and there followed a resounding smack, then a child's scream.

The conductor, giving a quick glance at the rest of Fred's papers, handed them back to him, his attention on the woman and child across the aisle. "You need help, ma'am?"

"Not at all, thank you. Children must learn to obey, you understand." Her voice rose above that of the howling child.

"Quite right." Turning, the conductor smiled at Fred and moved on to the next car.

Replacing his papers in their hiding place, he let out a tremendous sigh and whispered, "Thank You! Thank You, Lord!"

He slid down in his seat in a weary slump, only to remember Anna's package. Carefully he pried open one corner. Money! He investigated further. More money—in fact, that was all it contained. Securing the package again, he thought of how hard she had worked for what she earned. Possibly it represented every dollar she'd saved throughout her years of service. Probably all that she'd kept back was enough for her ticket from Baltimore to

New York.

He caressed the package with his fingers. More than a gift of love, it was a *sacrifice* of love. His heart went out to her over the ever-increasing miles between them.

Now, to the accompaniment of the train's lurching, his thoughts jumped back over the years, seeking out people and events that had placed him where he now sat. I'm sure if everything had been comfortable and painless for me I never would have wanted to be on this train today, he concluded.

Then into his musings came a jarring thought. For all the years he could remember he'd been straining toward filling his own needs and desires: for food, because he was frequently hungry; for clothing, because of the bitter cold of winter.

Forever, it seemed to him, he'd been reaching out for human comfort, for loneliness was usually his dismaying lot. It drove him to want to read, to beg for the answers to a million questions, to yearn for freedom to be himself instead of the slave of a master. He had drawn strength from the strong ones such as Grandma Betsy and Aunt Mary and Uncle Lawson.

The pattern of his life now became unbearably clear to him. Never had he thought of someone else's needs and desires above his own. Plainly Fred Bailey, the boy from Tuckahoe, had led a selfish, self-centered existence. Unlike Anna or Stanley, for instance, he had no personal knowledge of real sacrifice.

Gazing at Anna's package, he thought to himself, self-centeredness has been the worst part of my being a slave.

Then he prayed, "I'm making my first true sacrifice to You, Lord Jesus. I'm giving You my life, and no matter what it costs, I'll always do Your work. You know what I mean by that—I want 'to heal the brokenhearted . . . [and] set at liberty them that are bruised.' "

Fred smiled to himself then. While he knew there'd be little chance, as he sped on his way, of seeing mists with accompanying rainbows on such a bright September day, the promise he'd made to Heaven he'd hold securely in his heart as the most glorious of rainbows.

In New York, Fred arrived hungry, lonely, and unsafe. Remembering many warnings about unscrupulous people who might betray him and return him to Baltimore for the reward, he at first refused to ask for help or advice. Eventually he learned of David Ruggles, the secretary of the runaway-slave Vigilance Committee, who would, he hoped, provide him shelter and protection. For a time he searched in vain for Ruggles. But finally, in desperation, he confided his problem to a seaman who kindly took him to his home until he could locate the man.

Keeping her promise to see Fred in New York by mid-September, Anna arrived at the Ruggles home, where a man who had escaped from slavery years before married her and Fred.

They decided that for safety's sake the two of them should travel farther north immediately, to New Bedford, Massachusetts. There friends persuaded Fred to change his surname to hide his identity. He settled upon that of Douglass.

Needing to earn money, he began working on the waterfront, but again he found racial problems and changed jobs rather than bring attention to himself. He sawed wood, dug cellars, shoveled coal, swept chimneys, and worked at a candle factory and a brass foundry, while Anna did housework for other women.

In 1841, Mr. Garrison, a leading abolitionist, met Fred and influenced him to begin telling his story in public. But when Fred recounted his experiences as a slave, many in his audiences doubted his word, saying he was too well educated to be a runaway slave.

The criticism forced him to write the facts of his real identity and to whom he had belonged. It put him in constant danger of capture, especially with the announcement of future public appearances.

After the publishing of The *Narrative of the Life of Frederick Douglass* in 1845, Fred had to leave Anna and their children and flee to Great Britain, where he lectured constantly against slavery and prejudice. English Quakers raised money to purchase his freedom from Hugh Auld, to whom Thomas Auld had transferred ownership.

In 1847, Fred obtained his legal freedom. In the same year he established *The North Star,* an antislavery publication, in Rochester, New York; it continued until 1863.

It must have been a wonderful experience for Fred during those years to see his children well fed, comfortable in their home, going to school, and free to be the kind of people they chose to be. At the same time he headed the Rochester Underground Railroad, helping fugitive slaves by giving them shelter, food, and instruction on their way to freedom. Most of the fees he received from his lectures aided the fleeing slaves who came under his care.

Many years passed before Fred revealed the way in which he had escaped, for he wished to make sure those who had assisted him, as well as the conductor who had passed him that day on the train, would not suffer for their part in it.

Fred supported the women's rights movement of the day, besides being a leader in the antislavery crusade before and during the Civil War. He was instrumental in organizing two black regiments in Massachusetts, and he went to Washington to discuss problems of slavery with President Lincoln.

In 1871 he became assistant secretary of the Santo Domingo Commission. For a time he served as the District of Columbia marshal and then as recorder of deeds there. And from 1889 to 1891 he held the post of United States minister to Haiti. Out on the ocean, headed toward his new position in the West Indies, he must have thought back to those long-ago days when Daniel explained to him the course the great ships took from Chesapeake Bay to those far-off islands.

After a marriage of forty-four years, Anna died. Fred lived until February, 1895. He must have looked back many times during the later years of his life, remembering the way Providence had sent people into his life to encourage and help him reach the place in which he could serve the world best.